THE RED-GREEN AXIS

Refugees, Immigration and the Agenda to Erase America

By James Simpson

Dear Melo :   *8/11/17*

Thanks for your Support !

[signature]

CIVILIZATION JIHAD READER SERIES

Volume 4

ISBN-13: 978-1515085188

ISBN-10: 151508518X

The Red-Green Axis: Refugees, Immigration and the Agenda to Erase America is published in the United States by the Center for Security Policy Press, a division of the Center for Security Policy.

July 15, 2015

THE CENTER FOR SECURITY POLICY
1901 Pennsylvania Avenue, Suite 201 Washington, DC 20006
Phone: (202) 835-9077 | Email: info@securefreedom.org
For more information, please see securefreedom.org

Book design by Adam Savit
Cover design by Alex VanNess

TABLE OF CONTENTS

FOREWORD

For over twenty-six years, the Center for Security Policy has pioneered the formation and leadership of public policy coalitions to promote U.S. national security. The Center accomplishes this by working with past and present executive branch officials, key legislators, other public policy organizations, opinion-shapers in the media, and the public at large.

One of the most insidious aspects of the stealthy, subversive activities the Muslim Brotherhood calls "civilization jihad" is the collaborative partnership with the hard Left that enables it. We call this partnership the "red-green axis" – the conjoining of the socialist/communist radicals and the Islamic supremacists that has made the latter's efforts in the West considerably more successful than would otherwise likely be the case.

In this extraordinary study, investigative reporter Jim Simpson builds upon – and adds considerable detail to – the research conducted by Ann Corcoran. Her blog, Refugee Resettlement Watch, has become an indispensable resource for those concerned with the UN-directed and U.S. government-enabled colonization of America, all too often by unscreened aliens. Like Ms. Corcoran's monograph in this Civilization Jihad Reader Series, *Refugee Resettlement and the Hijra to America*, the present volume pulls back the curtain on a practice that has been going on for years with a view to, in President Obama's words, "fundamentally transform" America.

Mr. Simpson's copious documentation and fact-based findings chart the trajectory of the refugee resettlement industry. *The Red-Green Axis* illuminates the impetus that industry received early on via the United Nation's Human Settlement Policy – a plan to redistribute, not just wealth, but population and land. Mr. Simpson proceeds to show how this plan is being inexorably advanced by today's secretive and unaccountable federal refugee resettlement programs – operations that have brought nearly *2 million* refugees from Muslim nations to this country since September 11, 2001.

Of particular concern is the recently unveiled government-sponsored "Welcoming New Americans Initiative." Sixteen federal agencies and philanthropies and other private sector "partners" have been tasked with rewarding states and localities for accepting as "New Americans" erstwhile, and often unscreened, aliens. This public-private partnership is also focused on penalizing any who dare to resist the resettlement in their communities of such refugees.

Mass migration and colonization seeks to "erase America." It is enabled by myriad legal US immigration programs but most especially the refugee resettlement program, its contractors and subcontractors, left-wing philanthropies and activists. For those who love this country, its Constitution and freedoms, the picture Jim Simpson paints is alarming. It must be a catalyst for concerted action to prevent such an outcome. This monograph offers practical suggestions for mounting an effective resistance.

Frank J. Gaffney, Jr.
President and CEO
Center for Security Policy
2 July 2015

INTRODUCTION

As more Americans lose sleep with worry about the next Islamic terrorist attack on America, whether from a "lone wolf" or organized Jihadist cells, we may be missing the most certain source of danger: the rise of Muslim migration through federal immigration policy including our refugee and asylum programs and other US immigration channels.

America is being undermined by a tidal wave of immigration. Federal agencies collaborate with multinational entities and a universe of liberal organizations to bring in people from all over the world, while these so-called "Volunteer Agencies" (VOLAGs) are remunerated handsomely on taxpayer dollars.

Every year, the U.S. government allows approximately 1 million immigrants to establish legal permanent residence in the United States. Among them are people from countries very unfriendly to the U.S. About 140,000 emigrate from Muslim countries and an even greater number from communist countries.

Those are the *legal* ones. We have all witnessed the Obama administration's unconstitutional encouragement to illegal aliens as well. Last year 137,000 youths and families were welcomed into the United States following their illegal entry across the Southwest border, bringing crime, parasites and a deluge of exotic illnesses with them. People, including children, died as a result.[1] More illegals are already coming again this year. In 2013, the latest year for which data are available, the Department of Homeland Security (DHS) apprehended a total of 662,000 illegals, mostly at the southwest border.[2] Sixty-four percent came from Mexico, but tens of thousands arrived from hostile countries. Additionally, "inadmissibles" were stopped upon entering the U.S. at official border locations. This included 17,679 Cubans, 13,552 from Communist China, 2,618 from Russia and 2,882 from Ukraine.[3]

---

[1] James Simpson, "How an Obama Administration Policy is Destroying Lives," *Accuracy in Media*, October 16, 2014, accessed April 14, 2015, http://www.aim.org/aim-column/how-an-obama-administration-policy-is-destroying-lives/.
[2] John F. Simanski, "Annual Report Immigration Enforcement Actions: 2013, *U.S. Department of Homeland Security*, September 2014, accessed April 14, 2015, http://www.dhs.gov/sites/default/files/publications/ois_enforcement_ar_2013.pdf, 1.
[3] Ibid., 4.

Those are the ones we caught. Depending upon who is talking, border agencies capture somewhere between 30 and 90 percent of illegal border crossers. No one really knows how many they miss, but that range suggests at least 100,000 more per year. In 2005 Bear Stearns estimated the illegal alien population at roughly 20 million based on telltale evidence like increases in remissions to foreign countries, school enrollments and use of social services among border states.[4] The report cited an estimated cross border flow of 3 million in 2001, three times the legal amount.[5] If this represents a typical year, it would put the current illegal population at 40 to 50 million, not the absurdly low Census estimate of 11.5 million that politicians quote. Recall that Obama's DHS was printing 34 million green cards and work permits to accommodate his "executive amnesty."[6]

---

[4] Robert Justich and Betty Ng, CFA, "The Underground Labor Force is Rising to the Surface," *Bear Stearns*, January 3, 2005, accessed April 14, 2015, http://www.steinreport.com/BearStearnsStudy.pdf.
[5] Ibid., 11.
[6] David Martosko, "Up to 34 MILLION blank 'green cards' and work permits to be ordered ahead of Obama illegal immigrant 'amnesty'," *Daily Mail.com*, October 28, 2014, accessed April 13, 2015, http://www.dailymail.co.uk/news/article-2800356/us-immigration-authorities-prep-order-34-million-blank-green-cards-work-authorization-papers-obama-readies-executive-order-illegal-aliens.html.

THE REFUGEE PROGRAM

But while we are distracted by the wave of illegal immigration, an entire category of immigrant is being overlooked. And this group is having a profound impact on the complexion of our society – an impact that is rapidly rising to the level of a national security threat.

At last count, approximately 2,500 referrals from Syria had been received in 2014,[7] with 700 actually resettled so far. More will be received in this and subsequent years to help accommodate a significant proportion of the approximately 2.9 million Syrians fleeing civil war. On May 21, fourteen U.S. senators signed a letter urging President Obama to expand the refugee program to allow 65,000 Syrian refugees into the U.S. by the end of 2016.[8] This would require a dramatic increase in the current 70,000 annual cap on refugees, or force others to take a back seat to Syrians.

Because of the chaos in Syria, it will be virtually impossible to vet these people, according to the Federal Bureau of Investigation (FBI). How many will be members of the Islamic State (IS) or some other terrorist group or sympathetic to the jihadi cause? According to the FBI, IS supporters have already surfaced in the United States. As screening potential refugees for jihadist sympathies is strictly forbidden, how will we know if more supporters or even actual IS operatives arrive to join them?[9] In fact, Norwegian security recently discovered that some of the Syrian refugees chosen by the U.N. for resettlement in Norway are linked to IS and/or the al-Qa'eda-linked al-Nusra Front, or Jabhat al-Nusra.[10]

There is a plethora of special programs beyond the usual immigration process, including "diversity" visas, the refugee program, asylum seekers (asylees)

---

[7] "Proposed Refugee Admissions for Fiscal Year 2015: Report to the Congress," *U.S. Department of State, Department of Homeland Security and Department of Health and Human Services*, September 18, 2014, accessed April 14, 2015, http://www.state.gov/documents/organization/232029.pdf, iii.

[8] "Senators Urge President to Allow More Syrian Refugees to Resettle in U.S", *U.S. Senator Dick Durbin*, May 21, 2015, accessed May 23, 2015, http://www.durbin.senate.gov/newsroom/press-releases/senators-urge-president-to-allow-more-syrian-refugees-to-resettle-in-us.

[9] Chuck Goudie, "ISIS present in all 50 states, FBI director says:, *ABC 7 Eyewitness News*, February 25, 2015, accessed May 15, 2015, http://abc7chicago.com/news/isis-present-in-all-50-states-fbi-director-says/534732/.

[10] "UN quota refugees had terror links: Norway PST," *The Local NO*, June 2, 2015, accessed June 3, 2015, http://www.thelocal.no/20150602/un-quota-refugees-had-terror-links-norway-police.

and their families (follow to join). Refugees from Iraq and Afghanistan have their own program, Special Immigrant Visas (SIV). The table below shows the latest data from these various programs.

Refugees, Asylees and Other Special Categories

Category	2011	2012	2013
Refugees	56,384	58,179	69,926
Asylees	24,904	29,367	25,199
Follow to Join	9,550	13,049	13,026
SIV	719	3,312	1,902
Diversity Visa	50,103	40,320	45,618
Total	141,660	144,227	155,671

Sources: DHS/State Department Refugee Processing Center

Additionally, there are special programs for Cubans and Haitians that allow about 20,000 per year to emigrate to the U.S. with the same benefits awarded to refugees and asylees. There is even a "Rainbow Welcome Initiative" that funds a non-profit contractor (The Heartland Alliance International, LLC) to meet the special needs of lesbian, gay, bisexual, and transgendered (LGBT) refugees and asylees. Government funds 87 percent of this non-profit's $10 million annual budget. CEO Sid Mohn makes $330,000 per year in pay and benefits according to Heartland's 2014 tax return. Combined, the top four officers earn about $850,000 per year—almost all paid for by the U.S. taxpayer.

Finally, in 1991, the government created a "Temporary Protected Status" category to grant legal status in the U.S. to Salvadoran illegal aliens and others fleeing war or natural disaster in Central America. There are currently over 300,000 TPS aliens in the U.S. entitled to all the benefits of other legal permanent residents.[11]

While they are supposed to be "temporary," TPS enrollees simply re-enroll when their status expires. Most have been here since the 1990s. That status now applies to 11 countries. The Ebola-infected states of Liberia, Guinea, and Sierra Leone were added last year, and the latest, Syria, was added in January 2015.

---

[11] Lisa Seghetti, Karma Ester and Ruth Ellen Wasem, "Temporary Protected Status: Current Immigration Policy and Issues", *Congressional Research Service*, January 12, 2015, accessed April 25, 2015, http://fas.org/sgp/crs/homesec/RS20844.pdf.

Congress wrote the law to prevent TPS enrollees from obtaining green cards and sponsoring relatives for admission, but Obama has undermined this with Executive Orders.[12]

In December 2013, the Obama administration announced an in-country refugee program for Central American Minors (CAMs), allowing those under 21 years of age from Honduras, Guatemala, and El Salvador direct travel to the U.S. While those countries suffer high crime and poor economic conditions, afflicted populations do not rise to the definition of "refugee." By offering this status, the Obama administration is deliberately – and illegally – expanding the definition. It has been called a "rogue family reunification program"[13] and could see hundreds of thousands more coming in under its loose guidelines.

The refugee program is extremely expensive, but published numbers vastly underestimate the cost. The table below provides official estimates for resettling refugees, asylees, SIVs, and Cuban and Haitian program immigrants.

Estimated Funding for Refugee Processing, Movement and Resettlement ($ millions)

Fund	FY 2014	FY 2015
DHS Processing	$32.3	$32.9
State Dept. Admissions	$494.4	$418.0
HHS Resettlement	$616.3	$608.1
Total	$1,143.0	$1,059.0

Source: http://www.state.gov/documents/organization/232029.pdf

The costs of various social welfare benefits provided to these groups are not included in the above table. These costs are significant. The *2013 Office of Refugee Resettlement Report to Congress* estimated the percentage of refugees in the U.S. within the past five years currently using welfare services. These percentages were applied in the table below to totals for refugees and asylees as provided in the USCIS Yearbook of Immigration Statistics. Average per-user cost for each program was estimated based on enrollee data from the relevant federal agency and outlay numbers from Office of Management and Budget (OMB). Those per-person

---

[12] Jessica Vaughan, "Eroding the Law and Diverting Taxpayer Resources," *Center for Immigration Studies*, April 23, 2015, accessed May 10, 2015, http://cis.org/Testimony/Vaughan-Senate-Unaccompanied-Minors-042315.
[13] Ibid.

average cost estimates were then multiplied by the number of refugees and asylees. The resulting table below offers a rough, conservative estimate of refugee welfare costs.

Estimated Annual Welfare Costs for Refugees and Asylees

(Total Refugees/Asylees = 752,363)

	% Refugees	# Refugees	Avg. Annual Subsidy/User	Total Cost
Medicaid	56.0%	421,323	$4,083	$1,720,243,507
Cash Assistance (SSI only[1])	47.1%	354,363	$6,187	$2,192,610,222
Food Stamps (SNAP)	74.2%	558,253	$1,504	$839,724,683
Public Housing	22.8%	171,539	$9,202	$1,578,581,006
Total				$6,331,159,417

Sources: 2013 ORR Report to Congress; USCIS Table 6. Persons Obtaining Lawful Permanent Resident Status by Type and Major Class of Admission; FY 2009 – 2013

[1] Supplemental Security Income

So the refugee program could be costing the American taxpayer over $7 billion per year. But this is only part of the story. News reports last summer focused on unaccompanied alien children (UAC) flooding the southwest border. It went largely unreported however, that most were not unaccompanied. In addition to 68,541 UACs, another 68,445 families entered the U.S. in FY 2014 – for a minimum of 136,986, according to the Border Patrol. [14] 70,448 have been apprehended so far through April 2015.[15]

These illegals are excluded entirely from the refugee cost analysis, but their impact on the budget is substantial. This group was housed, fed and provided medical care until a permanent home could be found, whereupon they were relocated at taxpayer expense to communities throughout America. Under CAMs, they will be eligible for more.

---

[14] "Family Unit and Unaccompanied Alien Children (0-17) apprehensions FY 14 compared to FY 13", United States Border Patrol, Southwest Border Sectors, 2015, accessed May 1, 2015, http://www.cbp.gov/sites/default/files/documents/BP%20Southwest%20Border%20Family%20Unit s%20and%20UAC%20Apps%20FY13%20-%20FY14_0.pdf.
[15] "Family Unit and Unaccompanied Alien Children (0-17) apprehensions FY 15 through April", United States Border Patrol, Southwest Border Sectors, April 30, 2015, accessed May 10, 2015, http://www.cbp.gov/sites/default/files/documents/BP%20Southwest%20Border%20Family%20Unit s%20and%20UAC%20Apps%20-%20Apr_0.pdf.

Last year, President Obama requested $3.7 billion in additional funds to handle this influx, *over and above amounts appropriated in earlier years for UACs*. This year, relevant agencies, including ORR, DHS and DOJ have requested increases totaling $1.2 billion, however OMB estimated UACs would cost $2.28 billion in FY 2015.

When added together, the various refugee, asylee, SIV, Diversity, Cuban, Haitian, TPS and UAC programs are likely costing American taxpayers $10 billion or more per year, not the $1 billion claimed by the government.

WHERE IT ALL BEGAN

Over the past 50 years, the U.N. has devoted extensive resources to promoting population control. Educated Westerners listened and today this demographic is reproducing barely at replacement rates. We all thought this was the point. But now the U.N. is promoting what it calls "replacement migration." Because Western populations are reaching retirement age in large numbers, and because the U.N. now says the workforce cannot sustain itself without help, our population must be supplemented with those who never got the memo about containing population growth.

So after exhorting us to limit family size through abortion and birth control, the U.N. wants to backfill our declining populations with newcomers from countries where abortion and birth control are largely not practiced and often illegal. This is the kind of insanity that occupies the minds of the U.N. globalists.

But there is a method to their madness: *it is the Left's goal to build a "permanent progressive majority" ruling class.* The open borders agenda is the perfect vehicle. Millions of needy poor become bought and paid for Democrat voters once citizenship is obtained. And erasing American culture, traditions, and adherence to rule of man-made law inspires calls for still more government to solve the manufactured crisis. The more exotic and incompatible the immigrant population, the better, in some of their estimations. The threat posed by jihadis and our nation's other enemies does not concern the Left. The way some of them see it, such a threat will only serve to edge American society closer to anarchy and collapse. The Left envisions its cherished dictatorship of the proletariat rising from the ashes.

Many of the Left's really bad ideas are birthed in the United Nations. Drafted by Soviet agent-of-influence Alger Hiss, the U.N. Charter always envisioned a world body that would reflect Soviet global ambitions. The outlines of the open borders agenda were framed in the Vancouver Plan of Action at the 1976 U.N. Conference on Human Settlements.[16]

---

[16] "The Vancouver Action Plan: 64 Recommendations for National Action", *Habitat, U.N. Conference on Human Settlements*, May 31 to June 11, 1976, accessed, May 21, 2015, http://habitat.igc.org/vancouver/vp-intr.htm.

Being entirely socialist in intention and design, the U.N. envisioned redistributing not only wealth, but populations, across the globe. As stated in the document, "Human settlement policies can be powerful tools for the more equitable distribution of income and opportunities."[17]

Recommendations included:

- **A.1 National Settlement Policy:** All countries should establish as a matter of urgency a national policy on human settlements, embodying the distribution of population, and related economic and social activities, over the national territory.

- **A.2 Human Settlements and Development:** A national policy for human settlements and the environment should be an integral part of any national economic and social development policy.

- **A.3 More Equitable Distribution:** Human settlements policies should aim to improve the condition of human settlements particularly by promoting a more equitable distribution of the benefits of development among regions; and by making such benefits and public services equally accessible to all groups.[18]

The settlement provisions paid lip service to the notion of national sovereignty and property rights, for example, saying in Settlement policies and Strategies Preamble point 3, "The ideologies of States are reflected in their human settlement policies. These being powerful instruments for change, they must not be used to dispossess people from their homes and their land, or to entrench privilege and exploitation."

However point 1 in the preamble to the land section[19] makes clear the U.N. body's utter contempt for property rights. Point 2 emphasizes that land *must* be controlled by government:

1. Land, because of its unique nature and the crucial role it plays in human settlements, cannot be treated as an ordinary asset, controlled by individuals and subject to the pressures and inefficiencies of the market. Private land ownership is also a principal instrument of accumulation and concentration of wealth and therefore contributes to social injustice; if unchecked, it may become a major obstacle in the planning and

---

[17] "Vancouver Plan of Action, Recommendation A.4 More equitable distribution," *Habitat, U.N. Conference on Human Settlements*, May 31 to June 11, 1976, accessed, May 21, 2015, http://habitat.igc.org/vancouver/vp-a.htm.
[18] Ibid.
[19] "Recommendations from the Vancouver Plan of Action, June 1976, Section D, Land," *Habitat, U.N. Conference on Human Settlements*, May 31 to June 11, 1976, accessed, May 21, 2015, http://habitat.igc.org/vancouver/vp-d.htm.

implementation of development schemes. Social justice, urban renewal and development, the provision of decent dwellings and healthy conditions for the people can only be achieved if land is used in the interests of society as a whole.

2. Instead, the pattern of land use should be determined by the long-term interests of the community, especially since decisions on location of activities and therefore of specific land uses have a long-lasting effect on the pattern and structure of human settlements. Land is also a primary element of the natural and man-made environment and a crucial link in an often delicate balance. Public control of land use is therefore indispensable to its protection as an asset and the achievement of the long-term objectives of human settlement policies and strategies.

The U.N. justified these measures based on expectations about population growth, various environmental policies, and of course "social justice." These three concerns later morphed into the three "pillars" of the U.N. Agenda 21's Sustainability concept: environment, economy and social equity. It is merely socialism repackaged, but explains why the U.N. has now invented yet another oppressed class in need of resettlement: climate refugees.[20]

Who listens to all this garbage? Communist countries completely ignore the U.N. because the U.N. agenda is not meant for them. Think of Russia, China or Cuba resetting 10,000 Somali Muslims or 65,000 Syrians. Think again.

Only Westerners take these issues seriously so only Western nations implement U.N. policies at home. Unfortunately, the American Left treats U.N. edicts as Gospel, and the most fertile opportunities are found in the open borders agenda. The entire refugee/asylee agenda must be viewed as a U.N.-inspired plan *aimed at the West*, especially America, to erase borders and dilute Western culture through mass immigration from the world's failed nations. A corollary is that of the Organization of the Islamic Conference (OIC), whose 56 nations plus "Palestine" exercise disproportionate influence over the UN.[21] Its goal is to seed America and other Western countries with virulent Muslim groups who will not assimilate but instead attempt to dominate. With President Obama at the helm, that plan now has its greatest advocate.

---

[20] See: http://www.climaterefugees.com/Home.html.
[21] "CAIR and the Foreign Agents Registration Act", *Center for Security Policy*, March 1, 2010, accessed June 3, 2015, http://www.centerforsecuritypolicy.org/2010/03/01/cair-and-the-foreign-agents-registration-act/, p. 5.

REFUGEE CONTRACTORS

There are nine primary national contractors paid by the federal government to resettle refugees and asylees. These Voluntary Agencies or VOLAGS are listed below with their acronyms:

* *CWS – Church World Service*
* *ECDC – Ethiopian Community Development Council*
* *HIAS – Hebrew Immigrant Aid Society*
* *IRC – International Rescue Committee*
* *LIRS – Lutheran Immigration and Refugee Services*
* *CC/USCCB – Catholic Charities/U.S. Conference of Catholic Bishops*
* *USCRI – U.S. Committee for Refugees and Immigrants*
* *EMM – Episcopal Migration Ministries WRI World Relief Inc.*
* *WR – World Relief*

Additionally, there are 350 subcontractors in 190 cities all affiliated with the 9 main refugee VOLAGs, but cataloging them is beyond the scope of this paper.

Amounts awarded by the federal government to these 9 contractors since 2008 are shown in the table below. These data are likely incomplete because the contractors are often listed under more than one name or the name has been entered incorrectly.

Primary Refugee Resettlement Contractors ($ Millions)

	CWS	ECDC	HIAS	IRC	LIRS	CC & USCCB	USCRI	EMM	WR	TOTAL
2008	$28.7	$5.6	$11.5	$75.5	$24.6	$91.7	$6.8	$8.3	$17.8	$270.4
2009	$26.3	$6.8	$13.4	$101.0	$31.5	$127.0	$8.6	$10.5	$21.6	$346.7
2010	$37.9	$10.3	$16.3	$106.1	$34.8	$146.8	$17.8	$14.0	$24.2	$408.3
2011	$32.9	$11.4	$14.3	$101.7	$30.5	$220.4	$17.9	$12.1	$26.3	$467.5
2012	$38.7	$11.0	$15.5	$86.6	$35.0	$379.7	$31.5	$13.6	$24.3	$635.8
2013	$41.1	$13.1	$16.5	$84.1	$49.2	$360.0	$38.6	$14.9	$26.4	$643.8
2014	$45.9	$14.8	$17.7	$92.3	$56.0	$551.3	$40.3	$16.7	$33.1	$868.1
2015	$38.7	$12.8	$15.3	$57.2	$36.0	$145.0	$31.7	$15.2	$22.4	$374.1
TOTAL	$290.1	$85.6	$120.6	$704.5	$297.5	$2,022.1	$193.1	$105.2	$196.2	$4,014.9
Govt. Grants	$45.4	$16.3	$16.3	$305.5	$46.4	$104.7	$35.4	NA	$41.2	$611.2
Total Revenues	$79.8	$17.4	$31.2	$456.1	$50.4	$177.2	$39.2	NA	$58.5	$909.9
% Govt. Grants	57%	93%	52%	67%	92%	59%	90%	NA	70%	67%

Sources: USASpending.gov and IRS Form 990 Non-profit Tax Returns

Two more large contractors, Baptist Child & Family Services (BCFS) and Southwest Key Programs, Inc. (SW Key), focus primarily on unaccompanied alien children (UAC) and families. Many other small contractors – too many to catalog - are also involved in the UAC effort, and the VOLAGs have gotten into the game too. Combined they earned over $800 million in 2014. See the chart below.

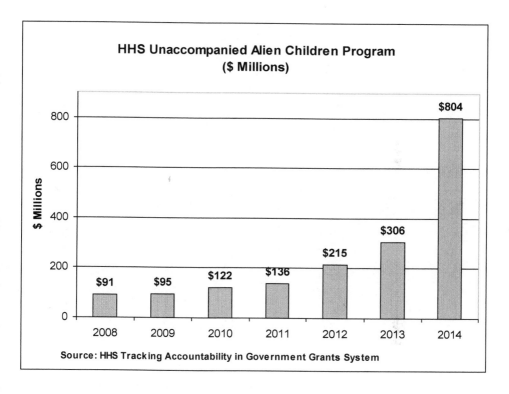

HHS Unaccompanied Alien Children Program
($ Millions)

Source: HHS Tracking Accountability in Government Grants System

There is some overlap in the refugee and UAC programs so these two charts cannot be combined. Suffice it to say however, that between them, the government is now spending well over $1 billion per year.

Because they are non-governmental organizations (NGOs), they can and do lobby for advantageous changes to law and build allies in Congress and the bureaucracy, all fertilized by an open spigot of taxpayer dollars. They could not pursue this agenda so aggressively were they government agencies.

The symbiotic relationship that develops explains why Obama and other big government politicians love such public/private "partnerships." For example, the recent Senate letter urging settlement of 65,000 Syrian refugees came at the behest of Refugee Council USA, a lobbying group representing the 9 VOLAGs and others in the resettlement business.

While 7 of the 11 contractors are affiliated with religious groups, the false notion that they are charitable organizations doing the Lord's work needs to be debunked. Many years ago, these VOLAGs may have used volunteers and provided funding for resettlement operations from private charitable donations and church tithes. Today, however, they are federal contractors, relying on the government for 76 percent of their income on average. Many receive virtually all their support from government. This is big business. Top management typically receives salary and benefit packages in mid-to-high six figures. They do the government's bidding, whether it honors religious principles or not.

Furthermore, the denominations represented all promote leftwing policies. Many reflect the "Social Gospel" i.e., the effort to marry socialist ideas with Christian doctrine. Many are directly or indirectly connected to communists and communist ideas like the so-called "liberation theology," a KGB creation, according to former Romanian intelligence chief, Ion Pacepa.[22]

Consonant with leftist strategies in all spheres, these organizations purposefully manipulate language—for example misnaming illegal aliens as "undocumented immigrants"—and subtly misinterpret Gospel to rationalize their advocacy. Then, with decidedly un-Christian vitriol, they savage anyone who questions their motives as "racists," "xenophobes," etc. And now, within their mission statements you will hear the newest refugee/immigrant mantra, "welcoming." More about that later. Following is a State Department map illustrating the VOLAGs' areas of operation.

[22] Ion Mihai Pacepa, "The Secret Roots of Liberation Theology", *National Review*, April 23, 2015, accessed May 15, 2015, http://www.nationalreview.com/article/417383/secret-roots-liberation-theology-ion-mihai-pacepa.

FY2014 Reception and Placement Program Affiliate Sites

CWS		LIRS	
EMM		USCCB	
ECDC		USCRI	
HIAS		WR	
IRC			

Source: Bureau of Population, Refugees, and Migration, US Department of State

935 11:23 STATE (INR)

THE VOLAG PROFILES

CHURCH WORLD SERVICE

(www.churchworldservice.org) – CWS is a subsidiary of the National Council of Churches, which was formed from the communist front Federal Council of Churches in 1950. The Federal Council was one of the early promoters of social gospel. That tradition was carried forward by the NCC where communist and socialist ideology found a natural home. NCC is today the U.S. subsidiary of the World Council of Churches, co-opted by the Soviet KGB in the 1970s.[23] The NCC also promotes Marxist liberation theology.

The NCC represents 37 denominations with 45 million people in over 100,000 U.S. congregations and has subsidiaries in all 50 states and the District of Columbia. The subsidiary Virginia Council of Churches' effort to place refugees in Hagerstown, MD, motivated Maryland resident Ann Corcoran to launch her now famous Refugee Resettlement Watch blog. This story is recounted in her e-book, Refugee Resettlement and the Hijra to America.[24]

NCC has been used as a vehicle to subvert American churches on behalf of the communist cause for decades. Parishioners would be shocked to know that their tithe dollars have supported communist guerrilla armies in Zimbabwe, Namibia, Mozambique, Angola, Nicaragua, El Salvador and elsewhere. CWS provided financial aid to the communist governments of Poland and Yugoslavia before the wall fell.[25]

The NCC strongly supports communist Cuba and normalization of relations. At the behest of the state-controlled Cuban Council of Churches, NCC assisted Cuba in demanding the return of Elian Gonzales, the Cuban refugee youth who escaped Cuba with his mother on a raft in 1999.[26] Unsurprisingly, the CWS is one of two VOLAGs primarily responsible for the Cuban/Haitian Entrant Program, and it doubtless coordinates with the Cuban Council. Some of these Cuban "refugees" are almost certainly intelligence agents, saboteurs and/or agitators, who join the refugee flow to establish bases in the U.S.

---

[23] Mark D. Tooley, "World Council of Churches: The KGB Connection", *FrontPage Magazine*, March 31, 2010, accessed May 5, 2015, http://www.frontpagemag.com/2010/mark-d-tooley/world-council-of-churches-the-kgb-connection/.

[24] Ann Corcoran, *Refugee Resettlement and the Hijra to America (Civilization Jihad Reader Series) (Volume 2)*, Washington: Center for Security Policy, 2015, http://www.amazon.com/Refugee-Resettlement-America-Civilization-Reader/dp/1508820708.

[25] "National Council of Churches", *DiscoverTheNetworks.com*, ? accessed, May 10, 2015, http://www.discoverthenetworks.org/printgroupProfile.asp?grpid=6916.

[26] "Some Frequently Asked Questions About The National Council of Churches and the Elian Gonzalez Case: How did the NCC become involved in the Elian Gonzalez case?", *NCCUSA.org*, ? accessed May 12, 2015, http://www.ncccusa.org/news/faq.html#qone.

NCC President Jim Winkler is a typical radical leftist. He called for impeachment of President Bush in 2006. He co-chaired the board of Healthcare Now! with steelworkers' president Leo Gerard, who advocated violence against tea partiers, and the socialist Quentin Young. Young was Obama's personal physician for 20 years, Obama's mentor on single-payer healthcare and his ideas formed the inspiration for Obamacare.[27]

Church World Service President and CEO is Reverend John L. McCullough. In 2014, he earned $288,000 in pay and benefits for this so-called charity work, according to IRS tax filings. Nice pay for a preacher.

It is no surprise to find CWS at the heart of the open borders crowd. It profits from the refugee program while the influx of refugees serves the Left's subversive agenda. In addition to revenue streams from government, CWS has received funding from Soros, Ford, Tides, the Vanguard Fund and many others. According to IRS tax filings, in FY 2014, CWS received $45.4 million in government grants, 57 percent of its total revenues.

CATHOLIC CHARITIES / U.S. CONFERENCE OF CATHOLIC BISHOPS

(www.catholiccharitiesusa.org) / (www.usccb.org) – These nominally Catholic organizations are the largest VOLAG, with hundreds of offices spread throughout the country. They are prominent members of the open borders/amnesty movement. The Catholic Campaign for Human Development (CCHD) is the grant making vehicle of the USCCB. It was founded in Chicago in 1969 with the help of radical organizer Saul Alinsky specifically to fund Alinsky's Industrial Areas Foundation (IAF).[28] CCHD has been a radical leftist funding vehicle ever since, giving millions to ACORN, the radical training school, Midwest Academy and others. IAF receives the largest percentage of CCHD grants of any CCHD grantee.[29] President Obama had this to say about CCHD:

> "I got my start as a community organizer working with mostly Catholic parishes on the Southside of Chicago that were struggling because the steel plants had closed. The Campaign for Human Development helped fund the

---

[27] "Quentin Young: The Quentin Young, Barack Obama Relationship", *Keywiki.org*, February 13, 2015, accessed May 12, 2015,
http://keywiki.org/Quentin_Young#The_Quentin_Young.2C_Barack_Obama_relationship.
[28] Matthew Vadum, "Left-Wing Radicalism in the Church: CCHD and ACORN" *Human Events*, October 26, 2009, accessed May 2, 2015, http://humanevents.com/2009/10/26/leftwing-radicalism-in-the-church-cchd-and-acorn/.
[29] Author unknown, "A Commentary on the Industrial Areas Foundation", *CatholicCulture.org*, ?, accessed May 15, 2015, http://www.catholicculture.org/culture/library/view.cfm?id=2885.

project and so, very early on, my career was intertwined with the belief in social justice that is so strong in the Church."[30]

USCCB founded the Catholic Legal Immigration Network, Inc., a $7 million subsidiary which assists illegal aliens based on "the Gospel value of welcoming the stranger." It aggressively promotes amnesty, believing that "all goods of the earth belong to all people. When persons cannot find employment in their country of origin to support themselves and their families, they have a right to find work elsewhere in order to survive. Sovereign nations should provide ways to accommodate this right."[31] USCCB has 270 field offices in 47 states. Board members include D. Taylor, president of the extreme left union, UNITE HERE!

Catholic Charities promotes liberation theology. It spread rapidly in Central and South America during the 1980s and was vigorously supported by certain Catholic denominations there. This explains much of the Central American Church's involvement with communist revolutionaries. During the Reagan administration, Catholic groups helped hundreds of thousands of Salvadorans to enter the U.S. illegally from the southern border. The Catholics' explicit purpose was to oppose President Reagan's foreign policy in Central America.[32] Unsurprisingly, USCCB is the other VOLAG managing the Cuban/Haitian Entrant program.

A good source for information about the Left's infiltration of our churches can be found at Exposing Marxism in the Church (www.religiousleftexposed.com) created by veteran investigative journalist, Cliff Kincaid.

There are hundreds of CC/USCCB chapters throughout the U.S. To catalog them all is beyond the scope of this paper. However, combined, they reeived $551.6 million from the government for refugee resettlement in 2014. Two of the largest Catholic Charities are Chicago (2014 revenues, $177.2 million) and Baltimore (2014 revenues $111.2 million). Combined, they received $159.1 million from government grants in 2014, 55 percent of total revenues. Catholic Charities has also received funding from United Way, Target, Gates, Global Impact, Robert Wood Johnson, Wal-Mart, and many others. Foundation Search found 17,505 grants since 1998. The top 500 totaled over $325 million.

---

[30] Vadum, op. cit.
[31] "Catholic Social Teaching, *JusticeforImmigrants.org*, ? accessed May 2, 2015, http://www.justiceforimmigrants.org/social-teachings.shtml.
[32] "Abstract: Chicago Religious Task Force on Central America Records, 1982-1992", *Wisconsin Historical Society*, ? accessed April 20, 2015, http://digital.library.wisc.edu/1711.dl/wiarchives.uw-whs-m93153.

(www.hias.org) – HIAS describes itself as a "major implementing partner of the United Nations Refugee Agency and the U.S. Department of State." HIAS claims to be the oldest refugee resettlement agency in the world. It provides pro bono legal services for Asylum applications and Removal hearings. Services include "Filings with USCIS, Representation at Asylum Interviews (Credible Fear Interviews, Reasonable Fear Interviews), Representation before the Immigration Court, Representation before the Board of Immigration Appeals (BIA), and Federal court appeals." HIAS lists its values as "Welcoming, Dignity and Respect, Empowerment, Excellence and Innovation, Collaboration and Teamwork, and Accountability."

HIAS President Mark Hetfield has spent most of his career in the immigration/refugee field, working for INS, as an immigration lawyer and as senior advisor on refugee issues at the United States Commission on International Religious Freedom. He is credited with transforming HIAS from a small agency focused on Jewish immigrants to "a global agency assisting refugees of all faiths and ethnicities." Hetfield earns $300,000 annually for a 35 hour work week, according to IRS filings. Donors include Vanguard and Tides Foundation. In FY 2013, HIAS received $16.3 million – 52 percent of total revenues – from government grants, according to the IRS.

In February 2013, HIAS published a report titled *Resettlement at Risk: Meeting Emerging Challenges to Refugee Resettlement in Local Communities.*[33] This report cited Ann Corcoran's Refugee Resettlement Watch blog as an example of the challenge resettlement organizations were beginning to face from citizens. The report recommends going on the warpath against Americans who resist utilizing the organized hate group Southern Poverty Law Center and the leftwing Center for New Community. WND's Leo Hohmann brought this report to light. It was commissioned by the J.M. Kaplan fund, whose Migration Program director, Suzette Brooks Masters, concurrently served as HIAS Trustee until June 2012, according to her LinkedIn page.[34]

---

[33] Melanie Nezer, "Resettlement at Risk: Meeting Emerging Challenges to Refugee Resettlement in Local Communities," *HIAS.org*, February 2013, accessed May 5, 2015, http://www.hias.org/sites/default/files/resettlement_at_risk_1.pdf.
[34] Leo Hohmann, "U.S. pushback against Muslim refugees 'growing'. Government contractor offers advice on how to quash dissent", *WND.com*, May 26, 2015, accessed May 26, 2015, http://www.wnd.com/2015/05/u-s-pushback-against-muslim-refugees-growing/.

Shortly after the report's publication, the Center for New Community published an *Islamophobia Movement in America* reference guide,[35] which includes Frank Gaffney, Brigitte Gabriel, Pamela Geller, Robert Spencer and others. This was followed one month later by another report titled Islamophobia, the New Nativism.[36] The report attempts to place blame for violent acts against immigrants, for example the Sikh Temple shooting, on the "racism, nativism, xenophobia, or Islamophobia" they claim is being inspired by opponents to this latest wave of immigration.

In November 2014, the White House announced a task force to examine "hate violence nationwide, including violence aimed at South Asian, Muslim, Sikh, Hindu, Arab, and Middle Eastern communities."[37] As related by SAALT (South Asian Americans Leading Together), the task force would build on the Matthew Sheppard hate crimes law. It is likely that this signals an official effort to begin targeting anyone opposed to the refugee/open borders agenda.

INTERNATIONAL RESCUE COMMITTEE

(www.rescue.org) – IRC is run by British Labor Party politician, David Miliband. His brother, "Red Ed" Miliband, Labor's pick for prime minister, lost in UK's most recent election. Miliband's father was a hardcore Marxist. While Miliband distanced himself from his father's extremist views, the apple doesn't fall far from the tree. As Environment Secretary under Tony Blair's Labor government, Miliband turned global warming into a primary policy agenda, seeking to make all private homes "carbon neutral," requiring nanny state compliance inspections. He warned British citizens that having "energy inefficient homes" would become "painful."

Miliband is advocating raising the refugee cap above 70,000 and resettling 65,000 Syrians in the U.S. despite the impossible task of vetting them for possible terrorist ties.[38] Miliband's position at IRC earns a cool half-million dollars for a 37.5 hour week of "rescue" work, according to its most recent IRS tax filing.

IRC and Miliband have friends in George Soros, the Clintons, and Samantha Power. Among others, IRC has received $1.2 million from Soros'

[35] "The Islamophobia Movement in America Reference Guide", *Center for New Community*, ? accessed May 26, 2015, http://newcomm.org/wp-content/uploads/2013/04/Islamophobia_America_Reference_Guide.pdf.

[36] "Islamophobia, the new Nativism", *Center for New Community*, 2013, accessed May 26, 2015, http://newcomm.org/wp-content/uploads/2013/05/Islamophobia-the-New-Nativism.pdf,

[37] "SAALT applauds task force to address Hate Violence", *Asian American Press*, November 7, 2014, accessed May 26, 2015, http://aapress.com/social-issues/racism-hate/saalt-applauds-task-force-to-address-hate-violence/.

[38] Bassem Mroue, "Aid Group Pressures U.S. To Resettle 65,000 Syrian Refugees By End Of Next Year", *Huffington Post*, April 9, 2015, accessed May 15, 2015, http://www.huffingtonpost.com/2015/04/09/syria-refugees-us_n_7036140.html.

Foundations and $2 million from the Ford Foundation over the past decade. IRC received government grants totaling $305.5 million FY 2013, 67 percent of 2013 revenues according to IRS tax returns. Government dollars dedicated to refugee resettlement were at least $92.3 million in 2014.

WORLD RELIEF, INC.

(www.worldrelief.org) – Initially founded in 1947 as *War Relief of the National Association of Evangelicals* to address humanitarian needs of post-war Europe, it was renamed World Relief in 1950. WRI describes itself as the largest evangelical refugee resettlement agency in America. It serves in "education, health, child development, agriculture, food security, anti-trafficking, immigrant services, micro-enterprise, disaster response and refugee resettlement." In FY 2014, WRI dedicated approximately 62 percent of program revenues ($32 million) to resettling and providing extended services to 13,508 refugees and legal assistance to 11,000 immigrants.

In keeping with Obama's "Welcoming" agenda, WRI has submitted its contribution in the form of a free PDF, *Welcoming the Stranger*.[39]

WRI is a member of The Immigration Alliance (TIA), a network of 30,000 churches that "provide critical immigration legal services to under-resourced immigrants." The Alliance also trains churches "to serve immigrants, coordinates and oversees efforts to ensure quality and consistency, and shares resources to maximize our effectiveness and reach." Other TIA member organizations include:[40]

- Anglican Church of North America

- Assemblies of God

- Baptist Convention of New York

- Christian & Missionary Alliance

- Christian Community Development Association

- Church of the Nazarene

- Converge World Wide

- Evangelical Covenant Church

- Evangelical Free Church

---

[39] This can be found at the website, www.welcomingthestranger.com.
[40] See: The Immigration Alliance, About Us, Membership, http://theimmigrationalliance.org/about-us/membership/.

- Free Methodist Church

- Foursquare

- Great Commission Churches

- Missionary Church

- National Latino Evangelical Coalition

- The Wesleyan Church

WRI received government grants totaling $41.2 million FY 2014, 70 percent of 2014 revenues according to IRS tax returns. $33.1 million of that went to refugee resettlement. Private foundation supporters include the Vanguard Charitable Foundation, Mustard Seed Foundation, Soros Fund Charitable Foundation, Pfizer Foundation, Global Impact and many others.

LUTHERAN IMMIGRATION AND REFUGEE SERVICE

(www.lirs.org) – LIRS has been involved in refugee resettlement for decades. Its 2013 tax return lists 17 Lutheran and many unrelated facilities nationwide receiving Refugee Resettlement grants from LIRS. Both HIAS and Catholic Charities are listed as recipients, so apparently these organizations cross-pollinate. In addition to refugee resettlement, LIRS has been actively involved in processing UACs.

LIRS CEO Linda Hartke served as chief-of-staff to former U.S. Rep. Chester Atkins (D-MA) in the 1990s. She later took positions with CWS and on NCC's board of directors. Her most recent post was director of the Geneva-based Ecumenical Advocacy Alliance. Linda wants LIRS to help create "communities of welcome" for illegals and refugees. Ms. Hartke earns $228,000 in pay and benefits according to tax returns.

LIRS receives funding from the Open Society Institute, the Ford Foundation, Global Impact, Fidelity Investment Fund, Bank of America Fund, Annie E. Casey Foundation and many others. The organization received $46.4 million, 92 percent of its income, from government grants in FY 2013.

U.S. COMMITTEE FOR REFUGEES AND IMMIGRANTS

(www.refugees.org) – USCRI formed as the International Institute in 1911, a brainchild of the YWCA, and became a VOLAG in 1977. Today, USCRI has 29 partner offices in 23 states dedicated to the needs of refugees and immigrants. It receives about 90 percent of revenue from government contracts. USCRI takes credit for inspiring the new CAMs program.[41]

President and CEO Lavinia Limón typifies the revolving door among VOLAG leaders. According to her USCRI biography, Limón served as the Director of the Office of Refugee Resettlement during the Clinton administration, "designing and implementing programs to assist newly arriving refugees in achieving economic and social self-sufficiency." She then moved to the National Immigration Forum where she directed NIF's Center for the New American Community.

Limón earns about $300,000 per year as CEO, according to USCRI's 2013 tax filing. But it is a family affair. Her brother, Peter Limón, made $140,000 as USCRI director of field offices that year.[42] One anonymous blog commenter who identified himself as a former USCRI employee says, "It's a family operation all right. I'm a former employee. As we used to say, 'When life gives you Limones... keep your head down and don't ask questions... or else...'"[43]

USCRI received $35.4 million in FY 2013, 90 percent of total revenues. It receives private funding from the Ford Foundation, California Community Foundation, Robert Wood Johnson, Nissan, the Oak Foundation, Western Union and others.

EPISCOPAL MIGRATION MINISTRIES

(www.episcopalmigrationministries.org) – Officially known as the Domestic & Foreign Missionary Society of the Protestant Episcopal Church USA. Repeating the "welcoming" mantra, EMM lists its first order of business as Welcoming Services: "Episcopal Migration Ministries' affiliate partners provide refugees with the information and services they require to thrive in their new communities within just months after arriving."

EMM does not provide non-profit tax returns so the proportion it receives from government is not known, however since 2008, EMM has received $105.2 million from the federal government for its refugee/immigrant work.

---

[41] "Central American Minors Program," USCRI, 2014, accessed May 10, 2015, http://www.refugees.org/our-work/refugee-resettlement/central-american-minors-program.html
[42] See: "U.S. Committee for Refugees and Immigrants, Inc.," IRS Form 990 *Return of Organization Exempt from Income Tax*, 2012, accessed June 2, 2015, http://www.guidestar.org/FinDocuments/2013/131/878/2013-131878704-0a20df5f-9.pdf, p. 7
[43] See: 1st comment by Anonymous at Peter Huston, "Is USCRI Albany a successful organization?" *PeterHuston*, May 6, 2011, http://peterhuston.blogspot.com/2011/05/is-uscri-albany-successful-organization.html.

(www.ecdcus.org) – The smallest of the VOLAGs, ECDC received $16.3 million from government contracts in 2014, 93 percent of total revenues. In addition, ECDC has received donations from the Open Society Institute, Komen Foundation, the United Way, Tides Foundation, even Citi Foundation (CitiBank), and others. In FY 2014, ECDC received $16.3 million – 93 percent of revenues – in government grants according to IRS tax filings.

ECDC testified before Congress last year that the UAC crisis could "lead to the demise of the refugee resettlement program as we know it."[44] This was primarily a funding concern given that virtually all of their revenue is derived from government contracts.

ECDC provides a wide variety of services to refugees, and is involved in other contractual services as well, for example SBA Microloans for new minority businesses.

SPECIAL GRANTS

ECDC's microloan program is an example of the myriad ways for VOLAGs to earn additional money by applying for special ORR grants limited only by one's imagination. [45] There are grants for building community gardens, home-based childcare and many others. An incomplete list of such grants and 2014-15 funding follows:

- Refugee Agriculture – (Community gardens) $1.0 million for 11 grants of about $85k each.

- Cuban Haitian – (Projects in localities most heavily impacted by Cuban and Haitian entrants and refugees); $18.7 million 13 grants, $16.5 million went to Florida)

- Ethnic Community Self Help – (Community building and cultural adjustment and integration) $6.1 million

---

[44] "Ethiopian Community Development Council, Inc. Testimony: Full Committee Hearing: Review of the President's Emergency Supplemental Request for Unaccompanied Children and Related Matters", *U.S. Senate Committee on Appropriations*, July 10, 2014, accessed May 10, 2014, http://www.appropriations.senate.gov/sites/default/files/hearings/UAC%20Hearing%20witness%20te stimony%20-%20ECDC.pdf.
[45] "Refugee Resettlement Programs", *Department of Health and Human Services, Office of Refugee Resettlement,* ? accessed May 25, 2015, http://www.acf.hhs.gov/programs/orr/programs/.

- Refugee Health Promotion – (Health screening, preventative care, other medical services) $4.6 million

- Individual Development Accounts – (Matched savings accounts to help refugees save for purchases) $4.3 million

- Microenterprise Development – (helps refugees develop, expand or maintain their own businesses and become financially independent) $4.4 million

- Microenterprise Development – Home-based Childcare (provides business opportunities to refugee women in a market where there is a shortage of childcare providers) $4.1 million

- Preferred Communities – (Preferred communities allow ample opportunities for early employment and sustained economic independence. In addition, they support special needs populations.) $12.5 million 18 grants.

- Refugee Social Services – (supports employability services and other services that address barriers to employment such as childcare needs, interpreters and social adjustment) Funding NA.

- School Impact – (Provides funding for activities that lead to the effective integration and education of refugee children) $14.8 million 36 states $410k avg.

- Services for Survivors of Torture – (Enables torture victims to regain their health and independence and rebuild productive lives) $9.8 million 31 grants $316k avg.

- Services to Older Refugees – (State grants ensure that refugees age 60 and above have access to mainstream aging services in their community) $3.3 million to 31 states, avg. $103k.

- Targeted Assistance – (Grants to states to help refugees obtain employment within one year's participation in the program) $4.7 million to 25 states, avg. $187k.

In addition to grant programs targeted specifically at refugees and refugee organizations, there is a plethora of grants available to all HHS contractors, including refugee/immigrant groups. For example, the Healthy Marriage Initiative provides grants to organizations providing marriage counseling and "Responsible Fatherhood" programs. For 2012, the latest data available, this initiative provided grants totaling $121 million. Many of the VOLAGs received these grants. Immigrant groups included:

- Cambodian Association of America, $570,000

- Creciendo Unidos, $359,796

- Immigrant and Refugee Community Organization, $492,000

UNACCOMPANIED ALIEN CHILDREN CONTRACTORS

BAPTIST CHILD AND FAMILY SERVICES

(www.bfcs.net) – BCFS is the granddaddy of resettlement for UACs. ORR 2014 grants totaled $280,156,954, strictly for "Residential Services for Unaccompanied Alien Children." One grant alone was over $190 million. BCFS does an astounding amount of work as a government contractor for HHS in many different areas, but this is obviously a growth industry for them. Last summer BCFS earned notoriety as the winner of a $50 million government contract to purchase Palm Aire Resort hotel in Texas and convert it to a 600 bed facility for illegals. The Resort featured indoor and outdoor pools, free Wi-Fi and cable. BCFS abandoned the contract following public outrage.

Palm Aire Resort Hotel

Texas-based BCFS partners with HHS, DHS, USAID, the Justice and Labor Departments and numerous Texas and other state agencies. BCFS receives almost all of its income through government grants – 90 percent in 2013, the latest year for which tax returns have been filed It received significantly more – at least $291.7 million – in 2014. (See VOLAG table above). Between 2001 and 2012, it also received at least $9,658,375 from private donors, of which over $8 million came from the following nine tax-exempt groups.

BCFS Top Private Funders

C.I.O.S.	$2,240,000
AT&T Foundation	$1,770,000
Mabee Foundation	$1,200,000
Eula Mae & John Baugh Foundation	$847,000
Goldsbury Foundation	$788,067
Kronkosky Foundation	$550,000
Cailloux Foundation	$424,000
Dan Graves Owen Foundation	$300,000
Meadows Foundation	$250,000
TOTAL	$8,369,067

Source: Foundation Search

C.I.O.S stands for "Christ Is Our Savior." Unlike most other nonprofits funding the illegal immigration agenda, this nonprofit really does appear to be genuinely concerned with truly charitable work. Perhaps it is in the early stages of takeover by the radical left, or is simply unconcerned about the open borders agenda.

SOUTHWEST KEY PROGRAMS, INC.

(www.swkey.org) – Southwest Key describes itself as an "Unaccompanied minors program" that serves "youth who enter the United States without parents or adult guardians and have been detained by immigration officials...." It operates 64 separate programs and has 2,000 employees in six states "impacting over 6,000 children and families on a daily basis." According to Southwest Key's website, their budget expanded to $150 million in 2013 for "new programs and shelters opening across the country to serve over 225,000 children and families."[46] Since DHS only reported 136,986 in 2014, about double the 2013 numbers, one wonders whose numbers are accurate. In 2014 the group received additional federal grants totaling over $122 million.

---

[46] Note: since this information was accessed on the SW Key website, it has been removed. But the Internet Archive retains the page: "About Us: Annual Reports and Financials", *Southwest Key Programs*, August 18, 2014, accessed May 31, 2015, https://web.archive.org/web/20140818014644/http://www.swkey.org/about/annual_report_financials.

Southwest is led by Dr. Juan Sanchez, who founded the organization in 1987. He earns $338,000 in pay and benefits. Dr. Sanchez's biography claims that he serves on the board of the National Council of La Raza, which may explain the Obama administration's largesse, given that domestic policy advisor Cecilia Muñoz is a former senior vice president of La Raza. Dr. Sanchez also claims to have received a "Rising to the Challenge Social Justice Award" from LULAC.

Government provides 98 percent of Southwest Key's revenue, $164.8 million in 2014, according to tax filings. Between 1999 and 2012, foundations contributed at least $3.1 million according to Foundation Search. Of this amount, over $2.8 million was provided by the following six donors.

Southwest Key Top Private Funders

Annie E. Casey Foundation	$1,025,336
Meadows Foundation	$761,000
J.P. Morgan Chase Foundation	$437,500
Houston Endowment	$250,000
Mabee Foundation	$250,000
National Council of La Raza	$103,000
TOTAL	$2,826,836

Source: Foundation Search

NETWORKING, PROPAGANDA & "CULTURE SHAPING"

Behind the federal spending, behind the primary religious and secular refugee/immigrant aid contractors, is a nationwide network of advocacy groups buoyed by billions in taxpayer and leftwing foundation dollars, focused on what they call "culture shaping." These organizations are all dedicated to resettling as many non-U.S. citizens as possible, entrenching them in our cities and towns, helping them prosper and eventually become voting U.S. citizens, while simultaneously softening up our society to accept them with open arms. The ultimate goal is to reshape America in the "progressive" mold, and most of these organizations admit it.

Starting in 2012, municipalities began celebrating National Welcoming Week.[47] For 2013's Welcoming Week, the White House recognized 10 Welcoming America Champions of Change. Outside of the immigrant/refugee/illegal alien advocacy community, few Americans have ever even heard of National Welcoming Week, but it is a major component of a nationwide "culture shaping" exercise to soften up America for growing waves of refugees and illegal aliens.

WELCOMING AMERICA

In November 2014, the White House announced creation of its Task Force on New Americans whose purpose would be to create, "Welcoming Communities and Fully Integrating Immigrants and Refugees."[48]

Sue Payne is a Maryland activist and co-host of Maryland Delegate Pat McDonough's radio talk show (WCBM AM 680 Baltimore). She listened in on an early Task Force conference call and heard participants explaining that refugees were to be considered "seedlings" to be planted in "receiving communities." She said:

---

[47] See a description at: http://www.welcomingamerica.org/2012/09/14/welcomingweek/.
[48] "Presidential Memorandum -- Creating Welcoming Communities and Fully Integrating Immigrants and Refugees," *The White House*, November 21, 2014, accessed April 21, 2015, https://www.whitehouse.gov/the-press-office/2014/11/21/presidential-memorandum-creating-welcoming-communities-and-fully-integra.

"As a listener on the call, it was easy to logically see how these communities would welcome immigrants out of the shadows, but also, it could be construed that the host community members might well be relegated into the shadows. In essence, the seedlings consume the host and what was once the original community is transformed."[49]

The Task Force is led by Domestic Policy advisor Cecilia Muñoz, a lifelong immigration activist and former National Council of La Raza senior vice president.

Mercedes Monteiro and father, RI Historical Preservation and Heritage Commission

My father emigrated from Cape Verde to RI so our family could build a better future

Read my story at WelcomingRI.com

Welcoming Rhode Island

ENRICHING NEIGHBORHOODS STRENGTHENING RI

The foremost NGO is Welcoming America, (www.welcomingamerica.org) which seeks to improve the image of immigrants, aliens and refugees to reduce local resistance to their presence or anticipated arrival. This is accomplished through the use of ads, billboards, social media, sympathetic news features, and direct "facilitated contact" between citizens and immigrant groups. According Welcoming America, "Research and practice have shown that direct contact is the most effective way to transform the way community residents think about immigrants and immigration."

Welcoming America seeks to soften up communities that are "pockets of resistance." [50] Communities resist however, for good reasons. Many of these "welcomed" refugees are turning towns into concentrations of open-ended welfare, crime, and no-go zones. Many refugees do not appreciate being "welcomed" either. For just one example, in the past two years, more than 20 Somalis settled in Minnesota have left to join IS, according to the FBI. Another seven have recently been charged with attempting to join. Two of them tried to pay their airfare with college loan money—almost certainly underwritten by taxpayers.[51]

---

[49] This information has been compiled from Sue Payne, a contributor to WCBM 680 and a Co-Host of the Pat McDonough Radio Show, *WCBM Talkradio AM*, February 26, 2015, accessed, May 20, 2015, 680http://www.wcbm.com/includes/news_items/1/news_items_more.php?section_id=1&id=478861.
[50] Ann Corcoran, "EEEK! 'Pockets of resistance' to refugee resettlement have developed; ORR hires 'Welcoming America' to head off   more" *Refugee Resettlement Watch*, June 15, 2013, accessed May 15, 2015, https://refugeeresettlementwatch.wordpress.com/2013/06/15/eeek-pockets-of-resistance-to-refugee-resettlement-have-developed-orr-hires-welcoming-america-to-head-off-more/
[51] Paul McEnroe, "Fraud charges added to ISIL terrorism case against 2 Twin Cities men", *Star Tribune*, May 19, 2015, accessed May 21, 2015, http://www.startribune.com/fraud-charges-added-to-terrorism-case-against-2-twin-cities-men/304258871/.

Following a successful "Welcoming Iowa" campaign in 2004, the Tennessee Immigrant and Refugee Rights Coalition (www.tnimmigrant.org) launched "Welcoming Tennessee" in 2006. It has since become the model for the nationwide effort. TIRRC received the National Council of La Raza's "Advocacy Affiliate of the Year" title in 2008.

Welcoming America is led by David Lubell, founder and former executive director of TIRRC.

Lubell is an Ashoka Fellow. Ashoka is an Arlington, VA-based, $60 million non-profit dedicated to creating "social entrepreneurs." According to its 2012-2103 annual report:

> David set up Welcoming America in 2009 to build a robust good receiving communities movement and create an enabling environment for more people and institutions to *recognize the role everyone must play in furthering the integration of recent immigrants* in the fabric of the U.S. (Emphasis added).[52]

Obama traveled to Nashville in December for a speech on immigrant rights and treated Lubell to a visit with him on Air Force One.[53] Obama's trip offered a window into the network of immigrant rights groups operating in just this one city. He gave his talk at Casa Azafrán, (www.casaazafran.org) a public/private-funded organization whose "resident partners" include:

- American Center for Outreach
- American Muslim Advisory Council
- Conexión Américas
- Family & Children's Service
- Financial Empowerment Center
- Global Education Center
- Justice for our Neighbors
- Mesa Komal Commercial Kitchen
- TIRRC
- United Neighborhood Health Services

---

[52] Ashoka Fellow David Lubell, http://usa.ashoka.org/fellow/david-lubell.
[53] "Obama honors immigrant rights leader David Lubell," *The Tennesseean*, December 9, 2014, accessed May 15, 2015, http://www.tennessean.com/story/money/2014/12/09/obama-honors-immigrant-rights-leader-david-lubell/20156983/

A search for Casa Azafrán on Guidestar produced the Tennessee Women's Theater Project. The connection is that TWTP presented a play, *Voices of Nashville*, "to explore Nashville's immigration experience from the point of view of its new Americans."[54]

The Tennessee Women's Theater Project is a small propaganda outfit funded by taxpayers. TWTP derived 100 percent of its 2013 income ($78,291) from government, and 70.8 percent in 2011. Their "Voices of Nashville" play was to tour during 2013-14.

WELCOMING AGENDA

Welcoming America's goal is to force Americans to accept mass immigration. Instead of addressing the problems created by immigrant populations that have no concept of our constitutional republic and no interest in assimilating, it engages organizations with a vested interest in immigration to improve messaging:

> David has identified a number of critical levers that, with low activation energy, can spark deep, scalable change. He is drawing in natural allies such as other organizations working on immigrant integration across the country and building a network of "welcoming" affiliates as implementing partners... In addition, he is working with municipal officials and influencing several federal government bodies to require that grantees working with immigrants engage receiving communities as part of their strategies. Understanding that media and advertising play a critical role in informing public opinion, he is also targeting these industries. Among other critical actors, David is beginning to work with corporations who have a vested business interest in making their communities more welcoming.[55]

Much of the Welcoming America agenda can be traced back to the Building New American Communities (BNAC) initiative, a three-year project funded by the Office of Refugee Resettlement around the turn of the 21st century.[56] ORR drove the effort to accommodate refugees and other immigrants and get them involved in the political process as soon as possible. Four principles guided this agenda:

1. New Americans should be involved significantly in decision-making processes;

---

[54] "Tennessee Women's Theater Project", IRS form 990, 2013, p, 2, http://www.guidestar.org/FinDocuments/2013/481/284/2013-481284622-0a0897ec-Z.pdf.
[55] Ashoka Fellow, op. cit.
[56] Brian K. Ray, "Building the New American Community: Newcomer Integration and Inclusion Experiences in Non-Traditional Gateway Cities", *Migration Policy Institute*, 2004, accessed May 12, 2015, http://www.ncsl.org/Portals/1/documents/immig/BNAC_Report1204.pdf.

2. Integration is a two-way process that implicates and benefits both new Americans and receiving community members;

3. Coalitions are among the vehicles that can foster effective and meaningful collaborations in order to tackle the numerous challenges and opportunities associated with socio-economic, cultural, and demographic change. These involve public-private partnerships that reach across levels of government and include a broad array of non-governmental organizations, as well as institutions and individuals from many different segments of society; and

4. Resources should be devoted to integration-focused interventions, as well as coalition building and training opportunities, which lead to systemic change.[57]

ORGANIZATION

Welcoming America is headquartered in Decatur, Georgia. Its latest non-profit tax return lists 2013 income of $1.2 million and net assets of $1.1 million. It received 6 grant awards from the Department of Health and Human Services between 2012 and 2014 totaling $443,758.[58] All six of these grants were under HHS's Fostering Community Engagement & Welcoming Communities program.

It also receives substantial funding from private foundations, according to Foundation Search, including the Kaplan Fund ($200,000 in 2011-2012), Ashoka, ($100,000 in 2012), Carnegie ($200,000 in 2013), Open Society ($300,000 in 2012), Unbound Philanthropy ($457,000 in 2011-2012), Starbucks ($50,000 in 2012), and others.

Welcoming America has a subsidiary project, Welcoming Refugees (www.welcomingrefugees.org). Its website claims, "Through a cooperative agreement with the Office of Refugee Resettlement, Welcoming America helps organizations and communities across the United States to prepare their communities for successful resettlement over the long term by fostering greater understanding and support for refugees."

Note that it says nothing about helping U.S. citizens cope with this added stress in their community, just how to make them more compliant.

WELCOMING AMERICA SUBSIDIARIES

[57] Ray, op. cit., ii.
[58] "Welcoming America," *Tracking Accountability in Government Grants System*, accessed April 21, 2015, http://taggs.hhs.gov/RecipInfo.CFM?SelEin=LCYqTyg%2FPE5IQTw7XlJaOEsK.

Welcoming America has 18 statewide and 52 city partners in 33 states and the District of Columbia. Instead of creating new organizations, the projects are administered by well-established advocacy groups that receive funding from national, state and local foundations and sometimes state and local government.

DETAILED EXAMPLES

Welcoming organization staffs are usually small, but regularly utilize a pool of volunteers, including college students, pro bono legal and other professional help that supplement staffing levels with government employees, and leverage their network of "partners" to have a much larger impact than their staff and budget alone could manage. A few examples follow.

Welcoming Alabama (www.welcomingalabama.com) has a presence in Auburn, Birmingham and Tuscaloosa and is the "immigrant welcoming project" of **Alabama Appleseed Center for Law & Justice, Inc.** (www.alabamaappleseed.org).

In operation since 2003, Alabama Appleseed is one of 17 independent state advocacy centers affiliated with the Washington DC-based Appleseed Foundation. Nebraska's Welcoming program, "Nebraska Is Home," (www.nebraskaishome.org) also uses an Appleseed subsidiary, Nebraska Appleseed (www.neappleseed.com/).

Alabama Appleseed utilizes pro bono legal help to carry out its mission. It is supported by numerous state and national organizations and foundations including:

- 43 Alabama law firms, including the Southern Poverty Law Center;

- 28 corporations, including AT&T, Wachovia Bank, BellSouth and Alabama Power;

- 29 foundations, including the Open Society Institute, Tides, Ford, Carnegie and AARP.

Alabama Appleseed 2013 revenues were $392,038 according to its most recent tax filings. Significant donors since 2008 include: Tides Foundation, $45,000; Public Welfare Foundation, $300,000; Mary Reynolds-Babcock Foundation, $470,010, Daniel Foundation of Alabama, $77,500 and Alabama Power Foundation, $65,000.

Welcoming California has two separate programs, both of which are sponsored by local government: "You, Me, We = Oakley!" (www.youmeweoakley.org) affiliated with the city of Oakley, CA; and "Redwood City Together," affiliated with Redwood City's 2020 project (www.rwc2020.org).

You, Me, We = Oakley has received $155,000 from the Y&H Soda Foundation since 2011. (See **Foundation Supporters** section of this report for more on Y&H Soda). Redwood's 2020 project cites numerous *Redwood City Together* supporters, including state and local government organizations, libraries, churches, the International Institute of the Bay Area and Welcoming America.

Welcoming Utah is a program of Comunidades Unidas (www.cuutah.org), a 16-year-old organization whose programs target the immigrant (mostly illegal alien) community. According to Mayra Cedano, CU's Community Engagement Programs Manager, Welcoming Utah engages immigrant parents about rights and responsibilities through meetings with charter school staff and Welcoming Week events throughout the community. University of Utah students are invited to participate, learn about programs and volunteer. The group also consults aliens as a DOJ Bureau of Immigration Appeals accredited agency to assist in applications for citizenship, Obama's Deferred Action for Childhood Arrivals (DACA), and other programs.

CU 2013 revenues were $317,000 according to IRS tax returns. Major funding comes from Komen Foundation, 275,300 2011-2013, to support CU's breast cancer and women's health programs. Komen has also donated to CASA de Maryland ($70,764 in 2014 and the Ethiopian Community Development Council $151,471).

Typical of welcoming organizations, CU is a small operation with 6 paid staff members but magnifies its influence with staff paid by Vista, Americorps and other government agencies. CU's unpaid Board is composed of prominent community leaders. Board member Diana Sanchez is Regulatory Learning & Administration manager for American Express Corporation. CU is further strengthened through a network of volunteer and Partner organizations, including:

- Welcoming America
- ACLU
- EPA (environmental justice grant for community civic education & clean up program)
- NCLR
- United Way (grant)
- AARP
- Public Interest Projects (NEO Philanthropy)
- American Express

- March of Dimes (grant)
- Utah Humanities Council

In-Kind Donors:

- Vista and Americorps paid staff
- Planned Parenthood
- Univision
- Utah Department of Health
- Others

Community Partners:

- Alliance Community Services
- Brain Injury Association
- Centro Hispano Provo
- The University of Utah's College of Nursing
- Community Health Centers (CHC)
- Guadalupe Schools
- Holy Cross Ministries
- Horizonte Instruction & Training Center
- Jackson Elementary School
- Lincoln Elementary
- Molina Healthcare
- National Alliance on Mental Illness (NAMI)
- Neighborhood House
- Rose Park Elementary
- Office of Diversity & Human Rights
- Salt Lake County Mayor's Office of Diversity
- Sorenson Unity Center
- South Valley Sanctuary
- University Neighborhood Partners
- Utah Health Policy Project
- Utah Nonprofits Association

- Utah Society for Environmental Education (USEE)

- Utahns Against Hunger

WELCOMING ECONOMIES (WE) GLOBAL NETWORK

Welcoming America's latest initiative is the WE Global Network. WE was launched publicly on April 15, 2015, the day after announcement of the White House Task Force on New Americans report, *Strengthening America by Welcoming All Residents.*[59] It emphasizes the alleged "economic development opportunities created by immigrants," especially in the rust-belt states.

It must have been under development for a while, as it is already a regional (but not global, or even national) network of 18 local governments in 10 states. Its efforts were identified in the White House report as "national best practice."

The WE Global Toolkit e-book[60] includes numerous chapters on how state and local governments can spend money to make it happen:

- Enhancing the Economic Contributions of International Students

- Establishing Welcoming Advisory Boards and Working Groups

- Integrating Highly-Skilled Immigrants and Refugees

- Resident Leadership Academies

- Seal of Biliteracy

- State-Funded Opportunity Centers

- State and Local Government Supported EB-5 Investor Visa Regional Centers

Global Detroit Executive Director Steve Tobocman said, "Communities across the country and around the world are in a *race to the top* to attract the human capital that will allow them to thrive in a global economy. Becoming a more welcoming place for immigrants gives us a leg up in that competition and helps us retain talented people of all backgrounds."[61] (Emphasis added).

---

[59] "Strengthening Communities by Welcoming All Residents: A Federal Strategic Action Plan on Immigrant & Refugee Integration", *The White House Task Force on New Americans*, April 2015, accessed May 25, 2015, http://www.welcomingamerica.org/wp-content/uploads/2014/07/Task-Force-on-New-Americans-Report-to-President-Obama.pdf.

[60] "Ideas that Innovate: State and Local Policies", *WE Global Network*, ?, accessed May 25, 2015, http://issuu.com/weglobalnetwork/docs/we_global_network_ideas_that_innova/1?e=0/12449822

[61] "We Global Network Launches Network for Immigrant Economic Development Initiatives Across America's Rust Belt," *WE Global Network*, April 15, 2015, accessed, May 25, 2015, http://www.welcomingamerica.org/wp-content/uploads/2015/04/WEGN-Press-Release_final.pdf

Race to the top? Where have we heard that before? Does Detroit really need to be spending more money, or will it receive federal funds for joining the *race to the top*, as state governments do through Common Core's *Race to the Top* fund?

NETWORKS FOR INTEGRATING NEW AMERICANS

Last year Obama announced an additional "seeding" initiative titled "Networks for Integrating New Americans (NINA)." NINA will be managed by World Education, Inc. and its partners, the National Partnership for New Americans, Community Science, Inc., IMPRINT, Network Impact, Inc. and of course, Welcoming America. The five networks[62] they will oversee are:

- White Center Promise, King County, WA
- We Rhode Island Network, Metropolitan Providence, RI
- Lancaster Refugee Coalition, Lancaster City and County, PA
- Idaho Refugee Community Plan, Boise, ID
- Central Valley Immigration Networks, Fresno, CA

Each of these umbrella organizations is actually a network of established public and private groups. For example, White Center Promise is comprised of the following:

- Highline Community College
- Highline Public Schools
- King County Housing Authority
- King County Library System
- One America
- Port Jobs
- Southwest Youth and Family Services
- White Center Community Development Association
- YWCA of Seattle-King-Snohomish

---

[62] "Networks for Integrating New Americans: Member Profiles", *World Education Inc.*, ? accessed May 24, 2015, http://worlded.org/WEIInternet/inc/common/_download_pub.cfm?id=14396&lid=3.

OTHER CULTURE SHAPING ORGANIZATIONS

There are numerous non-profit organizations dedicated to promoting refugee/immigrant "rights" and further pushing the "welcoming" narrative. Following are a few of the most prominent ones.

NATIONAL PARTNERSHIP FOR NEW AMERICANS

(www.partnershipfornewamericans.org) - Founded in 2010 NPNA's goal is to "achieve a vibrant, just, and welcoming democracy for all. We believe America's success is rooted in our ongoing commitment to welcoming and integrating newcomers into the fabric of our nation, and to upholding equality and opportunity as fundamental American values." According to its website, NPNA Partners include "12 of the largest statewide immigrant advocacy organizations in the country in order to leverage the existing immigrant integration work and expertise among member organizations for greater collective impact." These are:

- CASA de Maryland
- Causa Oregon
- Coalition for Humane Immigrant Rights of Los Angeles (CHIRLA)
- Colorado Immigrant Rights Coalition (CIRC)
- Florida Immigrant Coalition (FLIC)
- Illinois Coalition for Immigrant and Refugee Rights (ICIRR)
- Massachusetts Immigrant and Refugee Advocacy Coalition (MIRA)
- New York Immigration Coalition (NYIC)
- National Korean American Service & Education Consortium (NAKASEC
- OneAmerica (Seattle)
- Tennessee Immigrant and Refugee Rights Coalition (TIRRC)
- Voces de la Frontera (Milwaukee)

NATIONAL IMMIGRATION FORUM

(www.immigrationforum.org) - In operation since 1982, NIF describes itself as "one of the leading immigrant advocacy organizations in the country, with a mission to advocate for the value of immigrants and immigration to the nation." But "immigrant advocacy" largely refers to illegal aliens, *not* immigrants—so it is based on a lie. It advocates "birthright citizenship" without consideration for the legal status of the mother at the time of birth.

NIF promotes the "welcoming" mantra. Forum director Ali Noorani explains: "The Forum uses its communications, advocacy and policy expertise *to create a better, more welcoming America* that treats all newcomers fairly and respects the rights of all." (Emphasis added).

NIF claims support from "a network of conservative faith, law enforcement and business leadership," but its funding comes directly from the radical Left, including: Foundation to Promote Open Society (Soros): $4.1 million since 2009; Open Society Institute (Soros): $1.3 million since 2003; Ford Foundation: $4.6 million since 2001; Tides Foundation, $642,000 since 2010; Unbound Philanthropy, $400,000 since 2009, and many others.

EVANGELICAL IMMIGRATION TABLE

(www.evangelicalimmigrationtable.com) Describes itself as "a broad coalition of evangelical organizations and leaders advocating for immigration reform consistent with biblical values." These values include the following six principles:

- Respects the God-given dignity of every person

- Protects the unity of the immediate family

- Respects the rule of law

- Guarantees secure national borders

- Ensures fairness to taxpayers

- Establishes a path toward legal status and/or citizenship for those who qualify and who wish to become permanent residents

Even a cursory review of these "principles" reveals stark inconsistencies. For example, it is difficult to respect the rule of law, guarantee secure national borders and fairness to taxpayers while seeking to establish "a path toward legal status and/or citizenship" for illegal aliens. Such efforts only encourage more lawbreaking. Using a very slick video titled *The Stranger*, it advances the idea of "welcoming the stranger," comparing illegals to the plight of the Israelites in Egypt, when in fact unlike the Israelites, their circumstances are of their own making.[63]

The Stranger's "welcoming" theme is based on a fundamental lie. *Illegal aliens are not immigrants* – by definition they *cannot be*. An immigrant is defined as someone

---

[63] See: "The Stranger trailer," *YouTube.com*, July 9, 2014, accessed May 18, 2015, https://youtu.be/utmiJUmW8oI.

intent on settling where he has immigrated to. An alien is someone whose domicile is undefined. Illegal aliens are in America illegally and thus *cannot presume* to call America home. These self-proclaimed "evangelicals" are participating in a monstrous disinformation campaign that seeks to insinuate a Biblical basis for supporting the Welcoming America effort. It is designed to manipulate the emotions of well-meaning Americans but is in fact merely a naked rationalization for church-based groups to jump on the gravy train by supporting the Left's open borders agenda.

EIT is comprised of the following groups:

- World Relief Corporation

- Sojourners

- Council for Christian Colleges and Universities

- Bread for the World

- Ethics and Religious Liberty Commission

- Liberty Counsel

- National Association of Evangelicals

- National Hispanic Christian Leadership Conference

- National Latino Evangelical Coalition

- World Vision

- G92

G92

(www.g92.org) - Amnesty propaganda site for Christian youth. G92 takes its name from ninety-two references to the *ger*—the immigrant, in Hebrew—in the Old Testament. It describes itself as "a student movement that seeks to understand and respond to the challenges and opportunities of immigration in ways consistent with biblical values of justice, compassion, and hospitality." The G92 movement includes regular conferences, student groups on various campuses, and its website, formerly known as UnDocumented.tv, includes resources for campus groups, conference information and registration, videos, and a regularly updated blog.

Like many illegal alien advocacy groups, G92 uses ridicule, in this case by equating the criminal actions of illegal aliens with technically illegal things many do, like jaywalking. As with all leftist movements that pretend commitment to Christian principles, G92 perverts the meaning by twisting scripture and language to conform to the open borders agenda.

(www.ispu.org) – Claims to be "an independent, nonpartisan think tank and research organization committed to conducting objective, empirical research and offering expert policy analysis on some of the most pressing issues facing the United States." It declares its mission is to "provide expert analysis, insight and context to critical issues facing our nation, with an emphasis on those issues related to Muslim communities in the U.S. and abroad."

This organization's bias however, becomes immediately apparent upon closer inspection. Its report Manufacturing Bigotry, for example, promotes the Left's relentless narrative that efforts to preserve the rule of law and sanctity of marriage are prima facie evidence of bigotry:

> As certain groups—historically marginalized for their race, ethnicity/national origin, gender, sexual orientation, civic affiliation, or religious beliefs— become more visible, it is evoking a backlash from some who are eager to slow or reverse these groups' growing political and legal enfranchisement...
>
> To empirically measure the attempted disenfranchisement against these various groups, and links between efforts to roll back their rights, we examined bills in all 50 U.S. state legislatures from 2011 to 2013, across six issue areas: 1) Restrictions on abortion rights and access, 2) "Defense of Marriage Act" bills (DOMA) and other bans on same-sex marriage, 3) Right-to-Work legislation, 4) Anti-immigration proposals, 5) "Voter Identification" requirements, and 6) Anti-Sharia/Anti-"Foreign Law" bills (which serve as the report's legislative vehicle to measure Islamophobia).[64]

Not surprisingly, its Board of Advisors includes notorious leftist former congressman David Bonior (D-MI). Bonior is well remembered as one of President Reagan's key foreign policy opponents who vigorously defended the Nicaraguan communist Sandinistas. During his tenure, he was a member of the Congressional Progressive Caucus, the hangout for socialists and communists of every stripe. He was/is a member of Democratic Socialists of America. During the first Gulf war, he joined John Conyers and John Dingell to block FBI efforts to interview Detroit-area Muslims for counterintelligence purposes. In 2002 Bonior joined congressmen Jim McDermott (D-WA) and Mike Thompson (D-CA) on a fact-finding tour to Iraq that was financed indirectly by Iraqi intelligence[65]

---

[64] Saeed A. Khan and Alejandro J. Beutel, "Manufacturing Bigotry Community Brief," *ISPU.org*, November 10, 2014, accessed, May 20, 2015, http://www.ispu.org/content/Manufacturing-Bigotry.
[65] Steven Emerson, "Exclusive Photos Show Al Hanooti's Political Clout", *IPT News*, March 27, 2008, accessed May 10, 2015, http://www.investigativeproject.org/628/exclusive-photos-show-al-hanootis-political-clout#.

MAJOR FOUNDATION SUPPORTERS

Primary funding for the VOLAGs comes from the federal and state governments. However, a massive number of secondary and immigrant/refugee advocacy and assistance organizations are supported by wealthy state and national foundations with assets totaling tens if not hundreds of billions of dollars. Most of these well-established foundations are the Left's primary source of support outside government. In many cases initiated by families for genuine charitable purposes, these foundations have been infiltrated over time and captured by leftists who then turn the massive funding base to their agendas and political fellow travelers. Below is a sampling of the noteworthy radical Left foundations supporting the immigrant/refugee effort.

BAUMAN FOUNDATION

(www.baumanfoundation.org) – Grantees include a who's who of the radical left.[66] Director Patricia Bauman is a trust-fund leftist, also involved in other major radical left operations such as Catalist – which J. Christian Adams has called "Obama's database for fundamentally transforming America," [67] – Democracy Alliance, and the Brennan Center for Justice. She also advises J Street, the Soros-created Astroturf pro-Palestinian "Jewish" group. IRS filings report 2014 net assets of $84 million.

FORD FOUNDATION

(http://www.fordfoundation.org/) – Financed creation of the open borders movement and multiculturalism in the 1960s.[68] Funded creation and growth of the radical Mexican American Legal Defense and Education Fund (MALDEF), which spawned the DREAM Act concept, the National Council of La Raza (NCLR) and

---

[66] See Bauman's grantee list at www.baumanfoundation.org/grantees.
[67] J. Christian Adams, "'CATALIST': Obama's Database for Fundamentally Transforming America", *PJ Media*, September 17, 2014, accessed May 23, 2015, http://pjmedia.com/jchristianadams/2014/09/17/obamas-catalist-database/.
[68] William Hawkins and Erin Anderson, "The Open Borders Lobby and the Nation's Security After 9/11", *FrontPageMagazine.com*, January 21, 2004, accessed May 21, 2015, http://archive.frontpagemag.com/readArticle.aspx?ARTID=14499.

the Puerto Rican Legal Defense and Education Fund (PRLDEF), which gave us Supreme Court Justice Sonya Sotomayor. It is credited with turning the League of United Latin American Citizens (LULAC) from a conservative group that helped Hispanics assimilate into just another radical leftist Hispanic grievance group. Ford's impact on immigration activism cannot be overstated. Tax filings record 2013 net assets of $12.1 billion.

GILL FOUNDATION

(www.gillfoundation.org) – Founded by software billionaire Tom Gill, who along with Pat Stryker, another Colorado-based billionaire, provided most of the funding for the "Colorado Miracle" which turned the state from red to blue between 2004 and 2008. Their effort was dubbed The Blueprint, and inspired creation of the secretive, radical left funding operation, Democracy Alliance in 2005. Gill supports Welcoming America organizations in Colorado, Tennessee and Oregon. 2013 net assets, $234.4 million.

J. M. KAPLAN FUND

(www.jmkfund.org) – The Kaplan fund was created in 1945 by businessman Jacob Merrill Kaplan upon the sale of his business, the Welch Grape Company. Kaplan provided much funding for New York's New School for Social Research, America's counterpart to Germany's Marxist Frankfurt School for Social Research. Kaplan himself served as New School board chairman for 20 years. The Frankfurt School relocated to the Columbia Teacher's College in New York in 1933, when the school's Jewish communist professors were forced to flee Hitler's Germany.

The Kaplan fund's Migration Program provides "catalytic and early stage funding for a variety of innovative solutions to the integration challenges facing immigrants and refugees today. Notably, we support efforts to: engage receiving communities so they embrace the immigrants and refugees living in their communities…" Kaplan provided $200,000 to Welcoming America in 2011-12, and the funding for the HIAS report *Resettlement at Risk*. 2013 net assets, $143.1 million.

Migration Program director Suzette Brooks Masters has served on boards and/or worked for the Migration Policy Institute, the Open Society Foundation, the National Immigration Forum, HIAS, and others. Her LinkedIn page credits her with "launching the Receiving Communities Initiative with Welcoming America," and other immigrant/refugee related accomplishments.[69] She likely orchestrated funding for *Resettlement at Risk*.

NEO PHILANTHROPY

(www.theneodifference.org) – Formerly called *Public Interest Projects*, NEO spent $15.7 million in 2013 to "promote strongly aligned and effective immigrant rights organizations working to advance immigration policy and reform; immigrant civil engagement and integration; and defense of immigrant rights." This includes Alabama Appleseed ($50,000), the Arab Community Center ($100,000), the Border Action Network ($125,000), the Border Network for Human Rights ($390,000), CASA de Maryland ($270,000), the Colorado Immigrant Rights Coalition ($360,725), Comunidades Unidas ($15,000), Welcoming America ($89,000), TIRRC ($$469,000) Massachusetts Immigrant and Refugee Advocacy Coalition ($210,000) and many others. 2013 net assets, $19.6 million.

NEO's Board president is John Gilroy, Director of U.S. Public Lands with Pew Charitable Trusts. He also spent years with PIRG. V.P. Mark Colón is the Deputy Counsel of New York State's Division of Housing & Community Renewal. Board member Patricia Bauman also Directs the Bauman Foundation.

NEW WORLD FOUNDATION

(www.newwf.org) – NWF "seeks to build a progressive new majority for America..." NWF has provided $228,000 to Welcoming Colorado since 2011. NWF President Colin Greer joined the secretive Soros machine, Democracy Alliance, in 2014.[70] NWF Board Chair Kent Wong is director of the UCLA Labor Center, vice president of the California Federation of Teachers and a former SEIU attorney. Board member Don Hazen is the former publisher of Mother Jones and the current editor of AlterNet and the Independent Media Institute, both far left media organizations. NWF 2013 assets, $29 million.

OPEN SOCIETY INSTITUTE/FOUNDATIONS

(www.opensocietyfoundations.org) – Founded by George Soros, Open Society foundations support hundreds of radical non-profits and causes. Soros is a major open borders advocate. From 2010 to 2013, OSI provided $1.7 million to the

---

[69] "Suzette Brooks Masters," *LinkedIn*, ? accessed May 18, 2015, https://www.linkedin.com/pub/suzette-brooks-masters/1b/498/61.
[70] "Democracy Alliance", *Discover The Networks*, ? accessed May12, 2015, http://www.discoverthenetworks.org/printgroupProfile.asp?grpid=7151.

National Partnership for New Americans. Non-profit tax filings for various Soros foundatons include OSI 2013 net assets, $953.7 million; Foundation to Promote Open Society, 2013 net assets, $2.5 billion; Soros Fund Charitable Foundation, 2013 net assets, $280 million; Baltimore Open Society Institute (aka Alliance for Open Society International), 2013 net assets, $2.4 million.

PUBLIC WELFARE FOUNDATION

(www.publicwelfare.org) – A well-connected, long-established Washington, DC-based fund. It generously services a who's who of the radical Left including the Tides Center, the ACLU, Van Jones' Color of Change, the communist newspaper, In These Times, the radical Left Economic Policy Institute, the Blue Green Alliance (which is the renamed Apollo Alliance, a shady group of labor, environment, Democratic Party representatives that wrote Obama's stimulus), the Center for American Progress, and many more. 2013 net assets, $488 million.

PWF president is Mary McClymont. She previously served as board chair for the Migration Policy Center, national director for legalization at the Migration and Refugee Services of the U.S. Catholic Conference, president and chief executive officer of InterAction, the largest alliance of U.S.-based international development and humanitarian nongovernmental organizations (dedicated to the U.N.'s Sustainable Development agenda), various positions with the Ford Foundation, and trial attorney for the DOJ Civil Rights Division. She is the co-founder of Grantmakers Concerned with Immigrants and Refugees (www.gcir.org); was the chair of the board of the Migration Policy Institute; and served on the boards of Physicians for Human Rights, Amnesty International, the Advisory Committee of Elma Philanthropies Services and the Advisory Committee on Voluntary Foreign Aid, USAID. Currently, she serves on the board of the Washington Regional Association of Grantmakers and is a member of the New Perimeter Advisory Board.

UNBOUND PHILANTHROPY

(www.unboundphilanthropy.org) – Claims it is dedicated to "Welcoming newcomers. Strengthening communities." Its mission seeks to "transform long-standing but solvable barriers to the human rights of migrants and refugees and their integration into host societies…" Grant recipients include the National Immigration Forum, the National Immigration Law Center, the American Immigration Council, Tennessee Immigrant and Refugee Rights Coalition, Media Matters, Tides Foundation, the institutionalized hate group Southern Poverty Law Center and the radical Left Center for American Progress. Unbound financed the refugee propaganda film *Welcome to Shelbyville*.[71] Since 2008, Unbound has provided at least $2.4 million to the IRC, according to Foundation Search. 2013 net assets, $141 million.

VANGUARD CHARITABLE ENDOWMENT PROGRAM

(www.vanguardcharitable.org) – Vanguard is one of many donor-advised funds, which means that it channels donations to organizations of the donor's choosing, although in practice directors of donor-advised funds often recommend organizations and initiatives to support. Thus Vanguard has extensively supported immigration "reform" groups like Welcoming America. It provided over $22 million to the International Rescue Committee between 2005 and 2013. $1 billion income; 2014 net assets, $4.5 billion.

Y&H SODA FOUNDATION

(www.sodafoundation.org) – Typical of many state-based charities. Has provided $155,000 to welcoming projects in California since 2011; has also funded numerous other local immigrant organizations including, the International Institute of the Bay Area, which has its own "Immigrant Voices" program. The most prominent is East Bay Sanctuary Covenant, which claims to be "the largest affirmative asylum program in the country," representing over 500 asylum applicants per year. Through the Tides Center, Y&H supports the Arab Resource and Organizing Center. AROC provides legal and refugee/asylum application assistance to Bay area Muslims. Y&H donated about $500,000 in 2012 to its various immigration projects.[72] 2013 net assets, $129 million.

REYNOLDS LEGACY

MARY REYNOLDS-BABCOCK FOUNDATION AND Z. SMITH REYNOLDS FOUNDATION

These North Carolina-based foundations utilize legacy monies from the Reynolds Tobacco and Aluminum fortunes to fund radical left agendas and organizations, both in North Carolina and throughout the U.S. The Babcock

---

[71] Ann Corcoran, "Welcome to Shelbyville! The rise of a propaganda film", *Refugee Resettlement Watch*, January 15, 2011, accessed May 15, 2015, https://refugeeresettlementwatch.wordpress.com/2011/01/15/welcome-to-shelbyville-the-rise-of-a-propaganda-film/.
[72] See the Y&H 2012 grants list at: http://yhsodafoundation.org/resources/53/Final_2012_Grants_Awarded_.pdf.

Foundation has provided funds for numerous Welcoming America sponsors. 2013 assets, $182.4 million.

TIDES FOUNDATION

A pass-through fund which launders money for wealthy donors who want to support radical causes without being identified. R.J. Reynolds' granddaughter, Nancy Jane Lehman, co-founded Tides along with New Left organizer Drummond Pike. 2013 net assets, $142.3 million. Its sister fund, the Tides Center, was directed for years by ACORN founder and director, Wade Rathke. 2013 net assets, $68.2 million. Tides Center lists "support to resettle displaced Iraqi refugees," and to combat "inhumane immigration policy..." among its 2013 activities. Related organizations include the Tides Network, 2013 revenues, $13.7 million, Tides, Inc., 2013 net assets, $432,000, and Tides Two Rivers Fund, 2013 income, $2 million.

ARCA FOUNDATION

Extreme Left, Washington, DC-based fund which features prominently in the radical Left's immigration agenda. Founded by Nancy Jane Lehman's mother, Nancy Susan Reynolds – R.J. Reynolds' youngest daughter. It funds the Tides Foundation, the Center for American Progress, DEMOS, Media Matters for America, the Soros-created Jewish Astroturf organization J Street (which poses as a Jewish group but advocates the Palestinian cause), and the National Iranian American Council (NIAC), which Robert Spencer calls "the Mullah's Mouthpiece."[73] 2013 net assets, $55.7 million.

---

[73] Robert Spencer, "The Mullahs' Washington Mouthpiece?" *Discover the Networks*, July 8, 2009, accessed may 21, 2015,
http://www.discoverthenetworks.org/Articles/The%20Mullahs%20Washington%20Mouthpiece.html
.

WHAT IS TO BE DONE?

The Left has pursued the refugee/immigrant agenda for decades. While we were preoccupied with raising families and earning enough to support them, the Left has been working like termites to erase our culture, traditions, and rule of law from within. Even as its agenda threatens to destroy the nation we love, the open borders, unregulated immigration and refugee flow advocates revel in the chaos, poverty, and misery they create because it all serves their overriding objectives: power and wealth.

We are way behind the eight ball, but it is not too late for action. Aroused and outraged, Americans are finally beginning to wake up as they watch their communities transformed into third-world ghettos while jobs are taken, businesses undercut, pocketbooks emptied and taxes increased to pay for it all.

We must recognize that *there is no magic pill*. There are no easy solutions. We are in a war for our nation's survival, and we will all have to roll up our sleeves and get to work. Short of armed insurrection, the only answer is political. We can and must confront and change the political culture that has enabled open borders policies to gain such traction.

We need to confront and remove from office state and local officials who conspire with VOLAGs behind our back to shuttle in loads of aliens from third world venues. We need to elect principled leaders who will honor their campaign promises: seal the border, deport illegal aliens, abolish programs like Temporary Protected Status, Diversity Visas, and Special Immigrant Visas; modify or repeal the laws that have allowed VOLAGs to become immigrant/refugee advocates on our tax dollars, and rein in the many other forms of legal immigration that are deluging America with the world's problems and erasing our national character. Acknowledge and accept that *this is their agenda*! It is not just some mistake.

VOLAGS TARGET ACTIVISTS

Their own actions prove us right. Recent pushback by citizens against this unfettered flood of refugees, immigrants, and aliens has prompted the VOLAGs to develop a countering strategy that targets and seeks to discredit and attack anyone who questions the increasingly out of control Refugee Resettlement program. As noted earlier, the HIAS report *Resettlement at Risk* specifically mentions Ann Corcoran's Refugee Resettlement Watch blog:

> Online forums such as Refugee Resettlement Watch have emerged for individuals critical of the resettlement program to share their concerns. Many of the posts express disdain for the refugee resettlement program, particularly the resettlement of Muslim refugees, along with anti-Muslim views.

The report's recommendations follow:

- **Get organized.** Launch a funded, productive, organized initiative, coordinated nationally but strongly rooted in local action to raise awareness about the benefits of resettlement and "proactivity."

- **Develop a rapid-response team plan** that can respond to backlash quickly in communities facing or at risk of facing rising anti-refugee sentiment.

- **Conduct research on local anti-refugee leaders.** The national refugee agencies should partner with groups such as the Center for New Community and the Southern Poverty Law Center to learn more about individuals and groups leading local efforts to resist resettlement, to determine if they belong to organized anti-immigrant or anti-Muslim organizations or networks.

- **Monitor state legislatures** for anti-refugee bills and lobby accordingly.

- **The federal government should create national benchmarks** for refugee integration and measure progress toward success.

It is only a matter of time before Ann will appear on the Southern Poverty Law Center's "Hate Watch" list. This author already has. Of course the SPLC itself is a master of hate.[74] It manufactures it to defame anyone who challenges or even questions any aspect of the Left's agenda. The SPLC seeks to intimidate through public defamation. It is a form of psychological terrorism.

---

[74] James Simpson, "Southern Poverty Law Center: Wellspring of Manufactured Hate," *Capital Research Center*, October 7, 2012, Accessed May 21, 2015, http://capitalresearch.org/2012/10/southern-poverty-law-center-wellspring-of-manufactured-hate/.

The *Resettlement at Risk* report mentions a few of the higher-profile terrorism cases dealing with U.S.-based Iraqis and Somalis, but dismisses them as highly unusual. There are more such cases than they would like to admit, but they completely overlook the assimilation problems all immigrants and refugees, but particularly Muslims, bring with them. This author conducted a fact-finding trip to Lewiston, Maine a few years ago, where a large Somali refugee population had settled. Following were reports received from community residents:

- Kitchen cabinets were being used as indoor chicken coops;

- Inexplicably, bathtub and sink drains were deliberately plugged;

- Landlords were cited for code violations but could not repair the damage;

- The police blocked citizens' access to a city park frequented by Somalis;

- A woman pushing a baby carriage was chased out of the park by stick-wielding Somalis

- Somali men impregnate multiple Somali women then collect their welfare checks

- Other forms of welfare fraud abound

- Somalis demand interpreters even when they understand English. Other Somalis get paid for interpreting.

- Somalis call 9-11 complaining of chest pains, but then miraculously improve and walk off after the ambulance gets them downtown. If ambulance drivers refuse, they are sued.

Additionally, at least one Lewiston Somali later left to join IS and was killed.[75] Ann Corcoran's blog offers dozens of additional articles about Maine's travails. A Portland rental agent contacted for this report relayed these additional stories:

- One Somali family slaughtered goats in their kitchen and threw the carcasses in the back yard.

- Somalis who failed driving tests were taught to join letter-writing campaigns complaining about the test official who failed them. The Inspectors began passing all Somalis to avoid the stain on their records.

---

[75] Kathryn Skelton, 'These are not Muslims; they're monsters' Somali woman who grew up in Ethiopia talks about her ex-husband who joined ISIS and killed in Syria;" *SodereTube*, September 20, 2014, accessed, May 21, 2015, http://soderetube.com/2014/09/these-are-not-muslims-theyre-monsters-somali-woman-who-grew-up-in-ethiopia-talks-about-her-ex-husband-who-joined-isis-and-killed-in-syria/.

The agent observed that the refugees, no matter where they are from, arrive here with what they know. They are trained to take advantage of generous welfare benefits and to utilize tactics like the letter writing campaign, but *are not* taught how to assimilate. That can be blamed on the VOLAGs, their subcontractors, and the government agencies that oversee it all.

The National Lawyers Guild specializes in this kind of "help." For example, in collaboration with Maryland's illegal alien advocacy group, CASA de Maryland, NLG counsels illegals how to avoid capture and if captured what to do and who to call for help.

NEEDED RESPONSE

Americans concerned about this leftist, culture-destroying agenda must be armed with the facts and the methods to defeat it. Therefore, this report recommends a full-throated response borrowed from the Left's own strategy:

- **Get organized**. Develop a nationwide network of *paid* local activists.

- **Demand notification** from government officials before any resettlement effort.

- **Develop rapid-response teams** to block resettlements not preauthorized by citizens.

- **Conduct research on local VOLAG groups and subcontractors**. Identify and publicize the organizations and their leaders. Become familiar with their methods.

- **Monitor state legislatures** for objectionable legislation. Propose beneficial legislation

- **Demand assistance and support from city/state political leaders**. Identify friends and foes. Work to remove those unwilling to respond to citizen demands.

- **Demand assistance from Congressional representatives and senators.**

- **Expose the channels of corruption.**

Additionally, those state and federal elected officials who refuse to put American citizens first must be continuously identified and targeted for replacement. In the meantime, people must be more involved in the political process. Time and again, a motivated electorate has stopped objectionable action by calling their members of Congress and senators, attending hearings, and sometimes launching street protests. Recall Murrieta, California, last summer, when protesters succeeded in blocking DHS from planting illegals there. It's not easy and it's not fun, but if anyone has a better way, now is the time to become involved.

Other organizations dedicated to change have popped up all over the country. Would you like to assure cleaner elections? Join True the Vote (www.truethevote.org). TTV has state affiliates that train poll watchers and election judges throughout America. It has been so effective that it was deliberately targeted repeatedly by the IRS and other federal and state agencies – an action that culminated in TTV President Catherine Engelbrecht's gripping testimony before Congress.[76]

But you can effect change other ways as well:

- Does your church support any of the VOLAGs? Stop tithing, urge other members to do the same.

- Demand your pastor stop supporting such activities. If worse comes to worst, find another church.

- Many companies support the open borders agenda. Stop buying their products.

- Cancel subscriptions and refuse to read any periodical that supports open borders.

- Urge your congressional representatives and senators to defund the thousands of leftist non-profits that promote the open borders agenda on your taxpayer dime.

The Patriot's Handbook describes hundreds of ways to become actively involved in the battle to save our nation at any level of activity you choose.[77]

---

[76] See: "Catherine Engelbrecht gives a heart wrenching testimony", *YouTube*, posted February 12, 2014, accessed May 15, 2015, https://youtu.be/cISSoVIjyUc.
[77] James Simpson, *THE PATRIOT'S HANDBOOK: A Practical Guide to Restoring Liberty 2nd Edition, Revised [Kindle Edition]*, Baltimore: Self-Published, 2014, e-book, http://www.amazon.com/THE-PATRIOTS-HANDBOOK-Practical-Restoring-ebook/dp/B00LBNR5TO.

CONCLUSION

Lifelong Communist Angela Davis was recently filmed in Germany speaking with refugees who have taken over a school. The refugees have demanded that it be turned into a refugee-run community center. They demand "autonomy" but also expect government to front the funds necessary to run the facility "autonomously," by providing better food, healthcare, and housing than they apparently are already getting. They, as well as Davis, see this as entirely reasonable. The refugee leader says "we want a new life," as if that were justification for their actions.

Davis responds, "The Refugee movement is the movement of the 21st Century. It's the movement that is challenging the effects of global capitalism. It's the movement that is calling for civil rights for all human beings, so thank you very much and good luck with your work."[78]

This kind of thinking is already poisoning our body politic. Without strong and determined resistance, this form of "direct democracy," *e.g.,* rioting in the streets, will replace the rule of law with the rule of the fist. The time for action is *now.*

---

[78] Leo Hohmann, "Communist icon lets cat out of bag on U.S. 'refugees.' Lesbian touts 'movement of the 21st century'" *WND.com*, May 19, 2015, accessed May 21, 2015, http://www.wnd.com/2015/05/communist-icon-lets-cat-out-of-bag-on-u-s-refugees/.

Made in the USA
Lexington, KY
03 May 2017